ABT

W9-AEG-388

THE PORTLAND TRAIL BLAZERS

BY

MARK STEWART

Content Consultant
Matt Zeysing
Historian and Archivist
The Naismith Memorial Basketball Hall of Fame

NORWOOD HOUSE PRESS

CHICAGO, ILLINOIS

Norwood House Press
P.O. Box 316598
Chicago, Illinois 60631

For information regarding Norwood House Press, please visit our website at:
www.norwoodhousepress.com or call 866-565-2900.

All photos courtesy of AP Images—AP/Wide World Photos, Inc. except the following:
Rocky Widner/NBAE/Getty Images (cover);
Topps, Inc. (7, 14, 20, 21, 27, 30, 40 top, 43);
Author's Collection (16, 31, 34 both, 35 top left, 37);
Larry Berman/BermanSports.com (18, 19).
Special thanks to Topps, Inc.

Editor: Mike Kennedy
Associate Editor: Brian Fitzgerald
Designer: Ron Jaffe
Project Management: Black Book Partners, LLC.
Special thanks to Steve Baker and Brody vanderSommen

Library of Congress Cataloging-in-Publication Data

Stewart, Mark, 1960-
  The Portland Trail Blazers / by Mark Stewart ; content consultant,
Matt Zeysing.
     p. cm. -- (Team spirit)
  Summary: "Presents the history, accomplishments and key person-
alities of the Portland Trail Blazers basketball team. Includes time-
lines, quotes, maps, glossary and websites"--Provided by publisher.
  Includes bibliographical references and index.
  ISBN-13: 978-1-59953-126-7 (lib. bdg. : alk. paper)
  ISBN-10: 1-59953-126-7 (lib. bdg. : alk. paper)
  1. Portland Trail Blazers (Basketball team)--History--Juvenile litera-
ture. I. Zeysing, Matt. II. Title.
  GV885.52.P67S84 2008
  796.323'640979549--dc22

                                              2007010798

COVER PHOTO: The Trail Blazers celebrate a last-second game-winning shot during the 2002–03 season.

Table of Contents

SPORTS WORDS & VOCABULARY WORDS: In this book, you will find many words that are new to you. You may also see familiar words used in new ways. The glossary on page 46 gives the meanings of basketball words, as well as "everyday" words that have special basketball meanings. These words appear in **bold type** throughout the book. The glossary on page 47 gives the meanings of vocabulary words that are not related to basketball. They appear in ***bold italic type*** throughout the book.

BASKETBALL SEASONS: Because each basketball season begins late in one year and ends early in the next, seasons are not named after years. Instead, they are written out as two years separated by a dash, for example 1944–45 or 2005–06.

Meet the
Trail Blazers

Every basketball team, player, and fan begins each new season hoping for a winning record and dreaming of a chance to play for a championship. The Portland Trail Blazers and their fans expect nothing less. They may live and work in one of the smallest cities in the **National Basketball Association (NBA)**, but that does not keep them from thinking big.

Most NBA clubs start with one or two superstars and add players around them. The Trail Blazers look for players who will play as a team. Sometimes they have great stars, and sometimes they do not. As long as the Trail Blazers work together, however, the wins will come and the Portland fans will cheer.

This book tells the story of the Trail Blazers. They have a long history of success and are known for never giving up. Most important, the Trail Blazers understand that the key to achieving their goals is doing the little things it takes to win.

LaMarcus Aldridge congratulates Brandon Roy during a 2007 game.

Way Back When

In the late 1950s, the NBA decided to place teams on the West Coast. That gave a sports *promoter* named Harry Glickman a great idea. He started working to bring a team to Portland, Oregon. In January 1970, Glickman got good news. His city would be one of three to join the NBA for the 1970–71 season. Buffalo, New York and Cleveland, Ohio were the other two.

The Trail Blazers won their first game that season, against the Cleveland Cavaliers. They finished the year with 29 victories, including one over the 1970 champion New York Knicks and another over the Milwaukee Bucks, who would win the NBA Championship in 1971. Portland's best player was Geoff Petrie, a great shooter and scorer. Jim Barnett, a former star for the University of Oregon, also had a good year. So did guard Rick Adelman, who would coach the team many years later.

In Portland's second season, **rookie** Sidney Wicks joined Petrie to give the Trail Blazers two good scorers. The pair would often team up for more than 50 points a night. The Trail Blazers did not win many games, however, because they lacked a *dominant* center. They solved this problem in 1974 by **drafting** Bill Walton, who was an excellent defender and a terrific team player.

In 1976, the NBA added four teams from the **American Basketball Association (ABA)**. The rest of the ABA players were *distributed* among the NBA's other clubs. Portland received forward Maurice Lucas and guard Dave Twardzik. They blended almost perfectly with Walton and his teammates under the leadership of coach Jack Ramsay. Portland won 49 games in 1976–77 and went to the **playoffs** for the first time.

That spring, the Trail Blazers made it all the way to the **NBA Finals** against the powerful Philadelphia 76ers. Portland lost the first two games but won the next four to become league champions.

LEFT: Geoff Petrie rises to the basket for two points.   **ABOVE**: This trading card shows Bill Walton and Maurice Lucas setting up a play on offense. They worked together to bring Portland a championship in 1977.

Players such as Lionel Hollins, Johnny Davis, Bobby Gross, and Larry Steele helped make that team a very special one. The Trail Blazers were unselfish, and no one tried to be a star. Portland looked even better the following year, but an injury to Walton kept the team from returning to the NBA Finals. He was still named the league's **Most Valuable Player (MVP)**.

During the 1980s, Portland was led by Mychal Thompson, Jim Paxson, Calvin Natt, and Kiki Vandeweghe. The team's biggest star was the amazing Clyde Drexler. With help from Buck Williams, Jerome Kersey, Clifford Robinson, and Terry Porter, he guided the Trail Blazers back to the NBA Finals in 1990 and 1992. Adelman, Portland's former star, coached the team.

Although they did not win another championship, the Trail Blazers continued to be one of the NBA's best teams right into the 21st century. Portland also helped lead the way in bringing over players from Eastern Europe, including Drazen Petrovic and Arvydas Sabonis. From 1983 to 2003, the Trail Blazers reached the playoffs 21 years in a row.

LEFT: Clyde Drexler goes to the hoop against Michael Jordan during the 1992 NBA Finals.   **ABOVE**: Arvydas Sabonis soars high for a hook shot.

The Team Today

For most of their history, the Trail Blazers filled their **roster** with experienced players. When it came to the **NBA draft**, the team did not look for instant stars. Portland preferred to find players with good *potential*, and then slowly worked them into the starting **lineup**.

In recent years, the Trail Blazers began to follow a different path. They started a rebuilding program with many exciting young players. The new names included Brandon Roy, Jarrett Jack, Ime Udoka, Martell Webster, and LaMarcus Aldridge. The Trail Blazers believe the road to their next NBA Championship depends on their stars coming together as a team and reaching their potential.

Of course, with young players, a team can never be sure what will happen during a game. Sometimes the Trail Blazers put it all together and destroy their opponents. Other times they are on the wrong side of a *lopsided* score. However, no matter how a game starts, the Trail Blazers never give up and play hard right to the end.

Young stars LaMarcus Aldridge and Martell Webster enjoy playing for Portland's loyal and supportive fans.

Home Court

The Trail Blazers played their first 25 seasons in Portland's Memorial Coliseum. Fans loved going to games in the arena. Starting in the mid-1970s, the Trail Blazers had more than 800 sellouts in a row. In order to seat more fans, the team moved to a new home called the Rose Garden Arena for the 1995-96 season.

Portland is known as the "City of Roses." In fact, the Rose Garden Arena takes its name from the city's Rose Quarter neighborhood, which is located along the banks of the Willamette River. The river's climate is perfect for growing this type of flower. The Portland Rose Festival has been held every year since 1907. It features a parade with floats made of roses.

BY THE NUMBERS

- There are 19,980 seats for basketball in the Rose Garden Arena.
- As of 2007, the Trail Blazers have retired seven numbers: 13 (Dave Twardzik), 15 (Larry Steele), 20 (Maurice Lucas), 22 (Clyde Drexler), 32 (Bill Walton), 36 (Lloyd Neal), and 45 (Geoff Petrie).
- The Trail Blazers have also retired number 1 for their first owner, Larry Weinberg, and number 77 for coach Jack Ramsay, who led the team to the NBA Championship in 1977.

Team owner Paul Allen welcomes fans to the Rose Garden Arena.

Dressed for Success

In 1970, a contest was held to name Portland's new team. The most popular choice was "Pioneers," but a local college already used that name. The team decided to go with Trail Blazers instead. "Trail blazers" was a name given to pioneers who first explored the Pacific Northwest.

Portland's colors have been red, white, and black since the team's first season. In the 1990s, the Trail Blazers added silver. Their first uniform had the word "blazers" spelled out in lowercase letters across the chest. Later, the lettering stretched from the shoulder down to the waist. The Trail Blazers also added a bold stripe that curved from the shoulder down the leg of the shorts.

Portland's *logo* shows 10 lines meeting on a tilted rectangle. It is meant to be a modern symbol of the game of basketball. Some fans call it the "pinwheel."

Lloyd Neal models Portland's uniform from the mid-1970s.

UNIFORM BASICS

The basketball uniform is very simple. It consists of a roomy top and baggy shorts.

- The top hangs from the shoulders, with big "scoops" for the arms and neck. This style has not changed much over the years.

- Shorts, however, have changed a lot. They used to be very short, so players could move their legs freely. In the last 20 years, shorts have gotten longer and much baggier.

Basketball uniforms look the same as they did long ago … until you look very closely. In the old days, the shorts had belts and buckles. The tops were made of a thick cotton called "jersey," which got very heavy when players sweated. Later, uniforms were made of shiny *satin*. They may have looked great, but they did not "breathe." As a result, players got very hot! Today, most uniforms are made of *synthetic* materials that soak up sweat and keep the body cool.

Jarrett Jack shows off Portland's colors during a 2007 game. The team logo can be seen on his right pant leg.

We Won!

When the 1976–77 NBA season started, no one knew exactly what to think about the Trail Blazers. The season before, Portland had finished last in the **Pacific Division**. In its short history, the team had never had a winning record, and it had never made the playoffs. Still, the Trail Blazers had a lot of talent and potential.

After trading away Sidney Wicks and Geoff Petrie, Portland looked to Bill Walton as the team's leader at both ends of the court. Several good **role players**—Lionel Hollins, Bobby Gross, Lloyd Neal, and Larry Steele—were back for another year. New to the

team were Maurice Lucas, Dave Twardzik, Johnny Davis, Herm Gilliam, and Corky Calhoun. Lucas, a *burly* forward who had been a star in the ABA, was the most important addition. He became the team's top scorer.

Also new was Portland's coach, Jack Ramsay. It was his job to turn these players into a winning team. Ramsay convinced the Trail Blazers that the key to success was to be unselfish and hard-working. They discovered he was right when they won 22 of their first 29 games. The Trail Blazers finished the year in second place, with 49 victories. Almost every game was a sellout. "Blazermania" had begun.

How far could Portland go in its first trip to the playoffs? The Trail Blazers beat the defensive-minded Chicago Bulls in the first round. Next, they defeated the high-scoring Denver Nuggets. In the **Western Conference Finals**, the Trail Blazers swept the Los Angeles Lakers four games in a row. Portland fans had to pinch themselves to be certain this was not a dream. Their beloved Blazers were in the NBA Finals!

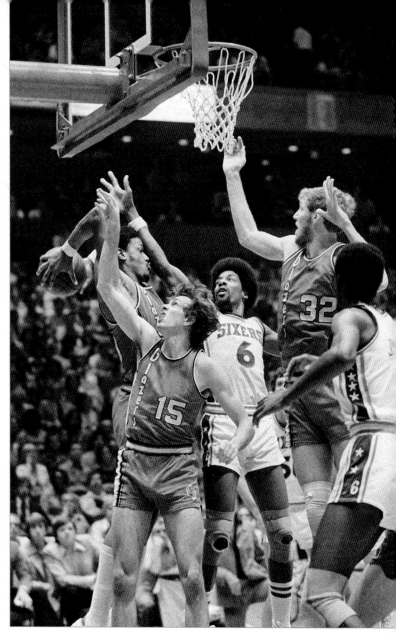

LEFT: Jack Ramsay   **ABOVE**: Maurice Lucas pulls down a rebound during the 1977 NBA Finals.

Few experts picked Portland to beat the Philadelphia 76ers. They had some of basketball's greatest stars, including Julius Erving, George McGinnis, Doug Collins, and World B. Free. The 76ers defeated the Trail Blazers in the first two games, but at the end of Game 2,

something strange happened. Philadelphia center Darryl Dawkins got angry and tried to punch a Portland player. He missed and hit Collins instead. Lucas stepped in and restored order. Suddenly, the 76ers did not look so tough.

The Trail Blazers beat Philadelphia badly in the next two games. Portland was quicker, smarter, and more aggressive. They continued to play well in Game 5 and won 110–104.

The Trail Blazers knew they would have a fight on their hands in Game 6. The 76ers were a proud team and did not want to lose four in a row.

The fans at Memorial Coliseum cheered the Trail Blazers as Erving and Walton dueled for 48 minutes. The 76ers' star scored 40 points. Walton responded with 20 points and also blocked eight shots and grabbed 23 rebounds. When the final buzzer sounded, the Trail Blazers were NBA champions, 109–107.

ABOVE: Bill Walton floats a shot over Darryl Dawkins of the 76ers.
RIGHT: Walton battles Julius Erving for a loose ball. Portland would not back down against Philadelphia.

Go-To Guys

To be a true star in the NBA, you need more than a great shot. You have to be a "go-to guy"—someone teammates trust to make the winning play when the seconds are ticking away in a big game. Trail Blazers fans have had a lot to cheer about over the years, including these great stars …

THE PIONEERS

GEOFF PETRIE   6' 4" Guard

- BORN: 4/17/1948   • PLAYED FOR TEAM: 1970–71 TO 1975–76

GEOFF PETRIE
TRAIL BLAZERS' GUARD

Geoff Petrie could score from anywhere on the court. He was taller than most guards and quicker than most forwards, so he usually had plenty of open shots. For more than 30 years, Petrie held the team record with 51 points in a game.

BILL WALTON   6' 11" Center

- BORN: 11/5/1952   • PLAYED FOR TEAM: 1974–75 TO 1977–78

The Trail Blazers used the first pick in the 1974 NBA draft on Bill Walton. When he was at his best, Walton was the league's top **all-around** center. Walton was an excellent passer, rebounder, and shooter. He was also a great defensive player.

ABOVE: Geoff Petrie   **RIGHT**: Maurice Lucas

MAURICE LUCAS　6' 9" Forward

- Born: 2/18/1952
- Played for Team: 1976–77 to 1979–80

Maurice Lucas was an **All-Star** in his final ABA season. The next year, his first with the Trail Blazers, he led the team in scoring, **offensive rebounds**, and minutes played. "Big Mo" gave Portland the extra power it needed to win the NBA Championship in 1977.

MAURICE LUCAS ▪ F

MYCHAL THOMPSON　6' 10" Forward/Center

- Born: 1/30/1955
- Played for Team: 1978–79 to 1985–86

Mychal Thompson was a smart, talented big man. He was a good shooter and rebounder and a beloved teammate. Thompson kept the Trail Blazers smiling—and winning—with his positive attitude and wonderful sense of humor.

CLYDE DREXLER　6' 7" Guard/Forward

- Born: 6/22/1962
- Played for Team: 1983–84 to 1994–95

Clyde "The Glide" Drexler was the most exciting star ever to wear a Portland uniform. He was a smooth and powerful player who always looked for ways to attack the basket. Drexler was most famous for his dunks, but he was also a superb passer, rebounder, and shot blocker.

JEROME KERSEY — 6' 7" Forward

• BORN: 6/26/1962 • PLAYED FOR TEAM: 1984–85 TO 1994–95

Jerome Kersey was known for his rim-rocking dunks, and he had a great personality to match his amazing jumping ability. Kersey's combination of power and enthusiasm made him a favorite of the Portland fans.

TERRY PORTER — 6' 3" Guard

• BORN: 4/8/1963

• PLAYED FOR TEAM: 1985–86 TO 1994–95

Terry Porter was an excellent leader who knew how to keep his cool when the pressure was on. He loved to have the ball in his hands with the clock winding down. In 1990, Porter set an NBA Finals record when he made 15 of 15 free throws in a game against the Detroit Pistons.

BUCK WILLIAMS — 6' 8" Forward

• BORN: 3/8/1960 • PLAYED FOR TEAM: 1989–90 TO 1995–96

The Trail Blazers had lost in the first round of the playoffs four years in a row before Buck Williams joined them. His rebounding, defense, and steady leadership helped the team reach the NBA Finals in his first season with Portland.

ABOVE: Terry Porter   **RIGHT**: Rasheed Wallace

CLIFFORD ROBINSON
6' 10" Forward

- BORN: 12/16/1966
- PLAYED FOR TEAM: 1989–90 TO 1996–97

The players quick enough to guard Clifford Robinson were not tall enough to stop his shot. The players tall enough to block his shot were too slow to stop his drives to the basket. This made Robinson a valuable weapon for the Trail Blazers, especially when he was coming off the bench.

RASHEED WALLACE
6' 10" Center/Forward

- BORN: 9/17/1974
- PLAYED FOR TEAM: 1996–97 TO 2003–04

Portland fans love players who show their emotions on the court, and they adored Rasheed Wallace. He led the Trail Blazers to the Western Conference Finals in 1999 and 2000.

BRANDON ROY
6' 6" Guard

- BORN: 7/23/1984
- FIRST SEASON WITH TEAM: 2006–07

Brandon Roy played in college in the Pacific Northwest, and he was very happy when the Trail Blazers picked him in the first round of the 2006 NBA draft. So were the Portland fans. Roy became the team's leader and best player in his first season.

On the Sidelines

Portland fans expect their team to reach the playoffs every year. For 21 seasons in a row, the Trail Blazers did just that. The coaches who led them to the playoffs included Jack Ramsay, Mike Schuler, Rick Adelman, P.J. Carlesimo, Mike Dunleavy, and Maurice Cheeks.

Ramsay, who coached Portland to the NBA Championship in 1977, is in the **Basketball Hall of Fame**. Adelman, who guided the Trail Blazers to the NBA Finals twice in the 1990s, was a member of the original 1970–71 Portland team. The coach of *that* club is still remembered around town. His name was Rolland Todd. He wore expensive boots, fur coats, and large hats. Everyone called him "Mod Todd."

In 1988, Paul Allen bought the Trail Blazers. Allen helped form the computer *software* company Microsoft with Bill Gates. In 2002, Allen competed in a hot dog eating contest at halftime of a Portland game. He ate his fair share but was no match for world champion Takeru "The Tsunami" Kobayashi.

Team owner Paul Allen gets a hug from one of his greatest players, Clyde Drexler.

25

One Great Day

The road to the NBA Finals can be a bumpy one. Every year but one after their magical 1976–77 season, the Trail Blazers made the playoffs but failed to reach the championship round. In 1990, they faced the San Antonio Spurs in the Western Conference semifinals. After six thrilling games, the series was tied at 3–3.

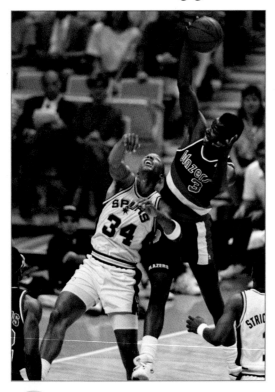

In Game 7, Portland was behind 97–90 with less than three minutes left. Once again, it looked as if the team would be making an early exit from the playoffs. The Trail Blazers, however, would not give up.

First, Kevin Duckworth, who was playing with a broken hand, made a jump shot. Next, Clyde Drexler, who had been ice-cold all game, swished a long **3-point shot** to cut the lead to 97–95. Portland then tied the score when Terry Porter passed to Jerome Kersey for a slam dunk. The crowd was buzzing as the game went into **overtime**.

With the score tied and less than a minute to play, the Spurs passed the ball to their star center, David Robinson. He had no room to shoot, so he flipped the ball to Rod Strickland, the team's point guard. Strickland whirled and threw a backward, over-the-shoulder pass—to no one!

JEROME KERSEY   F

Kersey was close to the ball and thought about letting it fly out of bounds. Then he saw Drexler standing with no one between him and the San Antonio basket. Kersey plucked the ball out of the air and threw it down the court. Drexler took the pass and swooped toward the basket. Strickland was so angry that he shoved Drexler from behind. The referee whistled him for a "breakaway foul."

Drexler made two free throws, and Portland was awarded the ball because of Strickland's dangerous play. Drexler was fouled again and made two more free throws. Portland went on to win the game 108–105. The confident Trail Blazers defeated the Phoenix Suns in the next round to complete their long road back to the NBA Finals.

LEFT: Clifford Robinson rises above the Spurs' Terry Cummings for a rebound during the 1990 Western Conference semifinals. Portland won that series and later moved on to the NBA Finals.   **ABOVE**: Jerome Kersey, whose quick thinking helped the Trail Blazers beat San Antonio.

Legend Has It

Which Portland team had the most "balanced" lineup?

LEGEND HAS IT that the 1998–99 Trail Blazers did. Nine different players led the team that year in nine different statistics. Isaiah Rider was the top scorer; Damon Stoudamire had the most

assists; Rasheed Wallace was the most accurate shooter; Walt Williams hit the most 3-point shots; Brian Grant had the most offensive rebounds; Arvydas Sabonis had the most defensive rebounds; Jim Jackson was the best free-throw shooter; Kelvin Cato averaged the most blocked shots; and Greg Anthony had the most steals.

Damon Stoudamire, Rasheed Wallace, and Brian Grant—three members of the 1998–99 Trail Blazers.

Who was Portland's best offensive rebounder?

LEGEND HAS IT that Clyde Drexler was. In the battle for rebounds, it is usually the centers and forwards who end up with the basketball. That was not true when Drexler was on the court. He was a master at grabbing offensive rebounds after one of his teammates missed a shot. Though he was a guard, Drexler would fly in and snatch the ball out of the air before the big men got their hands on it. During his career, Drexler averaged 2.4 offensive rebounds per game—more than any other guard in history.

Has an NBA team ever traded an office worker for a player?

LEGEND HAS IT that the Trail Blazers did. In 1982, they made a trade with the Indiana Pacers for a guard named Don Buse. Portland promised to give the Pacers a player in the future, but the two teams could never agree on which player that would be. Finally, the Trail Blazers "traded" their *marketing* expert, John Spoelstra, to Indiana. Spoelstra worked for the Pacers for 40 hours in return for Buse.

It Really Happened

The 1971–72 season was a long one for the Trail Blazers. The team won only 18 times and finished 51 games behind the Los Angeles Lakers in the **standings**. No team in NBA history had ever finished that far out of first place.

The fans who came to Memorial Coliseum for Portland's final home

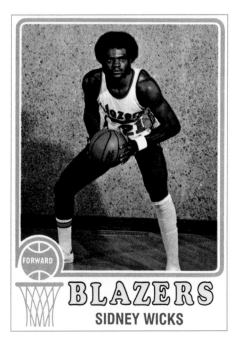

BLAZERS
SIDNEY WICKS

game in March 1972 did not expect a victory. The New York Knicks were in town. They were on their way to the NBA Finals, where they would meet the Lakers.

Sidney Wicks and Geoff Petrie were Portland's top scorers that season. The duo showed why in the first quarter when they outscored the entire Knicks team by themselves. When the period ended, the Trail Blazers led 32–16. The hot shooting continued in the second quarter, and by halftime Portland had a 63–31 lead.

In the second half, the Trail Blazers kept pouring it on. They scored 41 points in the third quarter and 29 in the fourth quarter.

Portland led the Knicks by more than 50 points late in the game. The final score was 133–86.

The Trail Blazers took 95 shots during the game and made 56. They had 60 rebounds to New York's 38. Wicks led all scorers with 30 points, and five other Portland players scored at least 12 points. Dale Schlueter ruled the backboards with 14 rebounds, and Larry Steele had eight assists.

The Trail Blazers may have been an imperfect team, but against the mighty Knicks they played a perfect game. Three nights later, Portland returned to reality. They traveled to Phoenix and gave up 160 points to the Suns!

LEFT: Sidney Wicks, who scored 30 points in Portland's victory over New York.   **ABOVE**: Dale Schlueter, the game's top rebounder.

EFFORT

Use of physical or mental
energy done through
exertion/achievement

REGARDLESS OF THE SCORE!

Team Spirit

Ever since the Trail Blazers won the 1977 NBA Championship, they have shared a special bond with Portland. The fans love the players and the team, and they rise to their feet after a great pass or courageous defensive play. In the years before the spacious Rose Garden Arena opened, it was practically impossible to find a ticket for a Trail Blazers game.

For nearly three decades, Portland fans who were unable to buy tickets listened to Bill Schonely describe the action on radio. He called the team's first **preseason** game in 1970 and was still on the air in the late 1990s. When the Trail Blazers were swishing their shots, Schonely would yell, "Rip City!" Soon this became a nickname for Portland itself.

Trail Blazers fans like to share their passion online. They have dozens of ***chat rooms***, ***blogs***, and fan sites. In 2007, the team decided to start a special website for people who love the Trail Blazers. It was the NBA's first site that helped fans meet each other.

Portland fans demand the best from their Trail Blazers. They are not shy about reminding the players what it takes to win a championship.

Timeline

The basketball season is played from October through June. That means each season takes place at the end of one year and halfway through the next. In this timeline, the accomplishments of the Trail Blazers are shown by season.

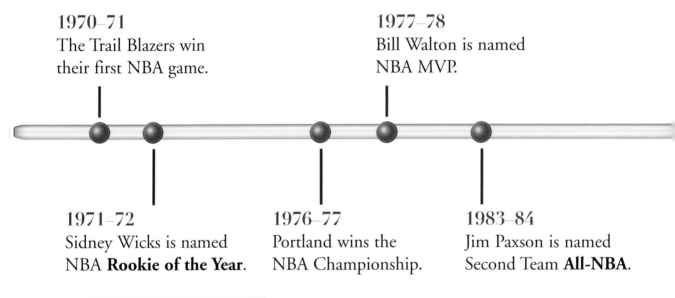

1970–71
The Trail Blazers win their first NBA game.

1977–78
Bill Walton is named NBA MVP.

1971–72
Sidney Wicks is named NBA **Rookie of the Year**.

1976–77
Portland wins the NBA Championship.

1983–84
Jim Paxson is named Second Team **All-NBA**.

Rick Adelman, a member of the 1970–71 team and later Portland's coach.

A pennant from the 1976–77 season.

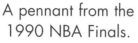

A pennant from the
1990 NBA Finals.

Rasheed Wallace
dunks during the
2003 playoffs.

1989–90
The Trail Blazers
reach the NBA Finals
for the second time.

1991–92
The Trail Blazers
reach the NBA Finals
for the third time.

2002–03
The team makes it to
the playoffs for the
21st year in a row.

1990–91
The team leads
the NBA with
63 victories.

1998–99
Mike Dunleavy is
named NBA
Coach of the Year.

2004–05
Damon Stoudamire
sets a team record with
54 points in a game.

Damon
Stoudamire
drives to the
hoop. He grew
up in Portland
rooting for the
Trail Blazers.

Fun Facts

MR. AMBASSADOR

In 1978, the Trail Blazers made Mychal Thompson the first player from the Bahamas to be the top pick in the NBA draft. He later served as the sports ambassador for his country.

LUKE, I AM YOUR FATHER

NBA forward Luke Walton is the son of Bill Walton. He was named in honor of his dad's friend and teammate, Maurice Lucas.

BRACE YOURSELF

In 1973, forward Terry Dischinger left the Trail Blazers to start a new career. He became an *orthodontist*. Dischinger is even more famous now. He lectures all over the United States.

THREE'S COMPANY

Clyde Drexler could do it all. He was just the third player in the NBA to finish his career with 20,000 points, 6,000 rebounds, and 6,000 assists. The first two were Hall of Famers Oscar Robertson and John Havlicek.

Larry Steele, Portland's most famous "thief."

NERVES OF STEELE

During the 1973–74 season, Larry Steele led the NBA in—what else?—steals! The following season, he set a team record with 10 steals in a game against the Los Angeles Lakers.

FINISH WHAT YOU START

When Jerome Kersey left Longwood College in 1984 to join the Trail Blazers, he was just two classes short of his *diploma*. Kersey returned to Longwood 22 years later and graduated as a member of the Class of 2006.

Talking Hoops

"Our fans are what makes coaching in Portland so special. The people truly love their team and their players."
— *Rick Adelman, on the thrill of being part of the Trail Blazers*

"From where I started, I never thought in my wildest dreams I'd make it in the NBA."
— *Terry Porter, on being drafted from a small college by the Trail Blazers*

"No one player can win or lose by himself."
— *Clyde Drexler, on why a superstar is never bigger than the team*

"The ball seemed to be moving from one end of the floor to the other so often I sometimes had trouble keeping up with it."
— *Sidney Wicks, on the biggest difference between college basketball and the NBA*

ABOVE: Clyde Drexler   **RIGHT**: Maurice Lucas and Bill Walton

"It was such a special time in a special town. Everything just had such a good vibration to it. The friendships forged in that time have lasted a lifetime."
—Bill Walton, on how the Portland players and fans came together in the 1970s

"The fans had fallen in love with us. Blazermania is what they called it … It was a great time for Portland."
—Maurice Lucas, on the support the Trail Blazers received from their home city

"It was very magical … We grew together as players and as human beings."
—Lionel Hollins, on Portland's championship team in 1976–77

For the Record

T he great Trail Blazers teams and players have left their marks on the record books. These are the "best of the best" …

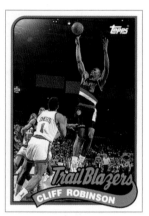

Clifford Robinson

TRAIL BLAZERS AWARD WINNERS

WINNER	AWARD	SEASON
Geoff Petrie	NBA co-Rookie of the Year	1970–71
Sidney Wicks	NBA Rookie of the Year	1971–72
Bill Walton	NBA Finals MVP	1976–77
Bill Walton	NBA Most Valuable Player	1977–78
Mike Schuler	NBA Coach of the Year	1986–87
Kevin Duckworth	NBA Most Improved Player	1987–88
Clifford Robinson	NBA Sixth Man of the Year	1992–93
Mike Dunleavy	NBA Coach of the Year	1998–99
Zach Randolph	NBA Most Improved Player	2003–04
Brandon Roy	NBA Rookie of the Year	2006–07

Brandon Roy powers to the hoop. He played with great confidence in his first season.

TRAIL BLAZERS ACHIEVEMENTS

ACHIEVEMENT	SEASON
Western Conference Champions	1976–77
NBA Champions	1976–77
Pacific Division Champions	1977–78
Western Conference Champions	1989–90
Pacific Division Champions	1990–91
Pacific Division Champions	1991–92
Western Conference Champions	1991–92
Pacific Division Champions	1998–99

ABOVE: Bill Walton waves to the crowd during a reunion of Portland's 1977 championship team.
LEFT: Zach Randolph, the NBA's Most Improved Player in 2003–04.

Pinpoints

The history of a basketball team is made up of many smaller stories. These stories take place all over the map—not just in the city a team calls "home." Match the pushpins on these maps to the Team Facts and you will begin to see the story of the Trail Blazers unfold!

TEAM FACTS

1 Portland, Oregon—*The Trail Blazers have played here since 1970.*

2 La Mesa, California—*Bill Walton was born here.*

3 Arkansas City, Kansas—*Lionel Hollins was born here.*

4 New Orleans, Louisiana—*Clyde Drexler was born here.*

5 Talbotton, Georgia—*Lloyd Neal was born here.*

6 Rocky Mount, North Carolina—*Buck Williams was born here.*

7 Darby, Pennsylvania—*Geoff Petrie was born here.*

8 Pittsburgh, Pennsylvania—*Maurice Lucas was born here.*

9 Albion, New York—*Clifford Robinson was born here.*

10 Milwaukee, Wisconsin—*Terry Porter was born here.*

11 Kaunas, Lithuania—*Arvydas Sabonis was born here.*

12 Sibenik, Croatia—*Drazen Petrovic was born here.*

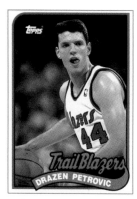

Drazen Petrovic

Play Ball

Basketball is a sport played by two teams of five players. NBA games have four 12-minute quarters—48 minutes in all—and the team that scores the most points when time has run out is the winner. Most baskets count for two points. Players who make shots from beyond the 3-point line receive an extra point. Baskets made from the free-throw line count for one point. Free throws are penalty shots awarded to a team, usually after an opponent has committed a foul. A foul is called when one player makes hard contact with another.

Players can move around all they want, but the player with the ball cannot. He must bounce the ball with one hand or the other (but never both) in order to go from one part of the court to another. As long as he keeps "dribbling," he can keep moving.

In the NBA, teams must attempt a shot within 24 seconds, so there is little time to waste. The job of the defense is to make it as difficult as possible for the offense to take a good shot—and to grab the ball if the other team shoots and misses.

This may sound simple, but anyone who has played the game knows that basketball can be very complicated. Every player on the court has a job to do. Different players have different strengths and weaknesses. The coach must mix these players in just the right way and teach them to work together as one.

The more you play and watch basketball, the more "little things" you are likely to notice. The next time you watch a game, look for these plays:

PLAY LIST

ALLEY-OOP—A play in which the passer throws the ball just to the side of the rim—so a teammate can catch it and dunk in one motion.

BACK-DOOR PLAY—A play in which the passer waits for a teammate to fake the defender away from the basket—then throws him the ball when he cuts back toward the basket.

KICK-OUT—A play in which the ball handler waits for the defense to surround him—then quickly passes to a teammate who is open for an outside shot. The ball is not really kicked in this play; the term comes from the action of pinball machines.

NO-LOOK PASS—A play in which a passer fools the defense by looking in one direction, then making a surprise pass to a teammate in another direction.

PICK-AND-ROLL—A play in which one player blocks, or "picks off," a teammate's defender with his body, then in the confusion cuts to the basket for a pass.

Glossary

BASKETBALL WORDS TO KNOW

3-POINT SHOT—A basket made from behind the 3-point line.

ALL-AROUND—Good at all parts of the game.

ALL-NBA—An honor given to the NBA's best players at each position at the end of the season.

ALL-STAR—A player selected to play in the annual All-Star Game.

AMERICAN BASKETBALL ASSOCIATION (ABA)—The basketball league that played for nine seasons starting in 1967. Prior to the 1976–77 season, four ABA teams joined the NBA, and the rest went out of business.

ASSISTS—Passes that lead to successful shots.

BASKETBALL HALL OF FAME—The museum in Springfield, Massachusetts where the game's greatest players are honored; these players are often called "Hall of Famers."

DRAFTING—Picking from a group of the best college players.

LINEUP—The list of players who are playing in a game.

MOST VALUABLE PLAYER (MVP)—The award given each year to the league's best player; also given to the best player in the league finals and All-Star Game.

NATIONAL BASKETBALL ASSOCIATION (NBA)—The professional league that has been operating since 1946–47.

NBA DRAFT—The annual meeting where teams pick from a group of the best college players.

NBA FINALS—The playoff series that decides the champion of the league.

OFFENSIVE REBOUNDS—Rebounds of shots missed by teammates.

OVERTIME—The extra period played when a game is tied after 48 minutes.

PACIFIC DIVISION—A group of teams that play in the region that is close to the Pacific Ocean.

PLAYOFFS—The games played after the season to determine the league champion.

PRESEASON—The practice games played before a season starts.

ROLE PLAYERS—People who are asked to do specific things when they are in a game.

ROOKIE—A player in his first season.

ROOKIE OF THE YEAR—The annual award given to the league's best first-year player.

ROSTER—The list of players on a team.

STANDINGS—A daily list of teams, starting with the team with the best record and ending with the team with the worst record.

WESTERN CONFERENCE FINALS—The playoff series that determines which team from the West will play the best team in the East for the NBA Championship.

OTHER WORDS TO KNOW

BLOGS—Online diaries; blog is short for "web log."

BURLY—Having a large, strong body.

CHAT ROOMS—Parts of a website that let people read and write messages.

DIPLOMA—A document given to a student who completes a course of study.

DISTRIBUTED—Divided among many.

DOMINANT—Ruling or controlling.

LOGO—A symbol or design that represents a company or team.

LOPSIDED—Extremely uneven.

MARKETING—Helping with the sales of a product or service.

ORTHODONTIST—A dentist who corrects irregularities in teeth, usually with braces.

POTENTIAL—The ability to become better.

PROMOTER—Someone who organizes events for the public.

SATIN—A smooth, shiny fabric.

SOFTWARE—The programs that help computers run.

SYNTHETIC—Made in a laboratory, not in nature.

Places to Go

ON THE ROAD

PORTLAND TRAIL BLAZERS
One Center Court
Portland, Oregon 97227
(503) 234-9291

NAISMITH MEMORIAL BASKETBALL HALL OF FAME
1000 West Columbus Avenue
Springfield, Massachusetts 01105
(877) 4HOOPLA

ON THE WEB

THE NATIONAL BASKETBALL ASSOCIATION   www.nba.com
  • *Learn more about the league's teams, players, and history*

THE PORTLAND TRAIL BLAZERS   www.trailblazers.com
  • *Learn more about the Portland Trail Blazers*

THE BASKETBALL HALL OF FAME   www.hoophall.com
  • *Learn more about history's greatest players*

ON THE BOOKSHELF

To learn more about the sport of basketball, look for these books at your library or bookstore:

  • Thomas, Keltie. *How Basketball Works.* Berkeley, CA: Maple Tree Press, distributed through Publishers Group West, 2005.

  • Hareas, John. *Basketball.* New York, NY: Dorling Kindersley, 2005.

  • Hughes, Morgan. *Basketball.* Vero Beach, FL: Rourke Publishing, 2005.

Index

The Team

MARK STEWART has written more than 20 books on basketball, and over 100 sports books for kids. He grew up in New York City during the 1960s rooting for the Knicks and Nets, and now takes his two daughters, Mariah and Rachel, to watch them play. Mark comes from a family of writers. His grandfather was Sunday Editor of *The New York Times* and his mother was Articles Editor of *The Ladies' Home Journal* and *McCall's*. Mark has profiled hundreds of athletes over the last 20 years. He has also written several books abot his native New York, and New Jersey, his home today. Mark is a graduate of Duke University, with a degree in History. He lives with his daughters and wife Sarah overlooking Sandy Hook, New Jersey.

MATT ZEYSING is the resident historian at the Basketball Hall of Fame in Springfield, Massachusetts. His research interests include the origins of the game of basketball, the development of professional basketball in the first half of the 20th century, and the culture and meaning of basketball in American society.